The Life OF
A RAMBLER

JUNE B. DEBATIN

I dedicate this book to my husband of 54 years,
Roger Debatin, who supported my career,
resulting in significant travel,
both in the US and internationally,
and after retirement, helped me
with my first book, which took some time.

ACKNOWLEDGEMENTS

Dr Dante Graves, cardiologist

Dr Ronald Derr, foot surgeon

Thomas Starling, friend and great supporter

Christie Prosser—I could not have finished the organisation
of the book without her skill and patience.

ABOUT THE AUTHOR

June B. Debatin was born on June 6th 1939 in Denver, Norfolk, England. She was the eldest child of three children, born to a Red Cross volunteer and a Royal Marine Commando, who served until post war England.

At 19, she moved to the United States and later, began her career in banking, finance, and investments. Eventually opening her own investment firm, June became a well-known face in the investment world and is considered a pioneer of international investing. After retirement she quickly rekindled her love for philanthropy, nature, and travelling. She spends much of her time with family and friends, attending church, or seeking a new ramble.

June is proof that adventures continue even into your 80s. She lives happily in her hilltop home in the scenic countryside of Middle Tennessee with her husband.

TABLE OF CONTENTS

ABOUT THE AUTHOR 7

INTRODUCTION: 1

  SCOTLAND, COLONSAY 1

  FROM COLONSAY TO ORONSAY 7

  A NEW ADVENTURE... 8

  EARLY SPRING 2016 13

  SUMMER 2016.. 14

  SEPTEMBER 2016.. 16

BEGINNING MY BIG ADVENTURE 19

  DAY 1: MONDAY 19

  DAY 2: TUESDAY FABLES OF OLD ENGLAND 21

  DAY 3: WEDNESDAY LAKES, FOLLIES, AND STONES 27

  DAY 4: THURSDAY THE KNIGHTS CASTLE 32

  DAY 5: FRIDAY, OUT ON THE CHASE 35

  DAY 6: SATURDAY..39

  DAY 7: SUNDAY 42

  DAY 8: MONDAY DORSET CIRCLES 50

  DAY 9: TUESDAY FRINGE OF THE FOREST.....................54

  DAY 10: WEDNESDAY DORSET MILLER 59

  DAY 11: THURSDAY...63

  DAY 12: FRIDAY INTO SOMERSET 65

  DAY 13: SATURDAY A KNIGHTS' QUEST.........................67

  DAY 14: SUNDAY 68

DAY 15: MONDAY 74

SEPTEMBER 2019, DINGLE, IRELAND..................................77

APPENDIX.. 81

HISTORY OF THE ISLANDS 83

    PART I: Colonsay 83

    PART II: Oronsay, Scotland 86

    PART III: Swallowcliffe Village 89

CHURCHES... 91

    ST MARY THE VIRGIN – EAST KNOYLE, WILTSHIRE 93

    ST JAMES – ANTSY PARISH CHURCH, WILTSHIRE 94

    SHAFTSBURY ST PETER'S DORSET 95

    ST PETER ad VINICULA – ST PETER IN CHAINS –
    TOLLARD ROYAL, WILTSHIRE...97

    ST MARY'S BREAMORE SAXON CHURCH, HAMPSHIRE
    98

    CORTON DENHAM ST ANDREWS CHURCH,
    SOMERSET 99

    MARNHULL, ST GREGORY, DORSET 100

    CHURCH OF ST MARY & ST BARTHOLAMEW,
    CRANBORNE, DORSET.. 103

AVON TYRELL 105

BOOKS THAT MAY INTEREST READERS AND WALKERS107

THE NATIONAL TRUST & THE ENGLISH HERITAGE 109

OPEN ACCESS LAND UK 112

THE DOMESDAY BOOK 114

THE WALKING MADONNA.. 116

THE POEM.. 117

INTRODUCTION:

SCOTLAND, COLONSAY

I was born in England at the beginning of the Second World War. The area I grew up in is not far from the coast, and during those war years, many airbases were opened, both British and US. We were a small family: my mother and father, and my sister, Joy. Years later, I met a young man from the US, and we got married. As young as I was, I had never travelled far from my home and certainly had never been on a plane. Life changed then, and as is often said, "The rest is history." One thing was certain: I missed the things I had loved: green fields, lanes along which there grew wild roses, and all types of wildflowers. Many, many years later, I would never have imagined how, for a little while, I was able to walk and enjoy the places and things I loved.

Fast forward, in 2005, my sister, then living in England, and I, in the US, were discussing places we might enjoy a week's vacation. Since we lived in different countries, the opportunity to be together for a week meant a lot to us. However, we are quite different. I like walking or hiking, and Joy likes beaches and warm weather. While warm weather is nice, it has little bearing on my walks.

This year, several travel options were considered. Colonsay was chosen after reading *'The Crofter and the Laird,'* a book by John McPhee, researching the islands, and finding a long and interesting history. Colonsay is part of a chain of islands in the Atlantic Ocean off the west coast of Scotland. The island measures approximately two miles wide and 12 miles long. Colonsay's history dates to the Mesolithic period around 500 BC and includes numerous Bronze Age sites that were once occupied.

To travel to Colonsay, it is necessary to get a ferry to the island. We caught the ferry in Oban, a seaside town on the west coast of Scotland. We learned it was also necessary, if we were to stay on the island, we would need to find accommodation. We did just that and were very happy there. The gentleman of the house had received culinary training in Glasgow, and the food was great. The trip to Colonsay took 2.5 hours. However, we were warned high tides could delay the ferry either way and with bad weather, we might have to stay on the island until the ferry could get in. As it was, the weather was good. Since we had only a week, we decided to walk around, ask questions, and see what suited us. Fortunately, this fit both Joy and me.

Although Colonsay has some high hills, we did not seek out those areas. We found old sheep trails that were great. In some places, however, they were a little narrow and close to the edge. Sheep trails went both uphill and downhill. I loved the variety, the upside-down trails and wind in my hair.

One day, we walked about 6 miles, mostly on sheep trails and carrying in my backpack a nice, packed lunch from our landlord. This walk gave me a new appreciation of the island, especially as when we were there, flowers were blooming. I was very surprised to see wild roses, honeysuckle, heather, and small yellow iris. Considering that the Atlantic most certainly had storms big enough to do damage to trees and fauna, I was amazed they continued to survive.

During our stay, Kiloran Bay provided tranquility from our busy jobs. Scotland's beaches are known for their cleanliness, and Kiloran beach is an example of a wide expanse of clean white sand. While we were there, it was remote with few visitors. It is easy to forget one is in Scotland. The island also featured beaches that might cause one to think this was not Scotland.

The charm of Colonsay lies not only in its natural beauty but also in its storied past. The island has a rich history dating back thousands of years, with evidence of human habitation from the Mesolithic period. Colonsay's strategic location made it an important site during various periods of history, including the Viking invasions and the tumultuous times of the Highland Clearances.

As we explored the island, we were captivated by the remnants of ancient structures, such as the Bronze Age sites and old stone circles. These historical markers stand as silent witnesses to the island's past, connecting us to the people who once lived there and their way of life.

Our days were filled with leisurely walks along the sheep trails, which offered stunning views of the Atlantic Ocean and the surrounding islands. The trails varied in difficulty, with some leading uphill to panoramic vistas, while others meandered through valleys, adding splashes of colour to the rugged landscape. One day, carrying a backpack of great sandwiches, as I walked, I wondered how these flowers and other fauna survived.

There are two cemeteries on Colonsay, one dating back to the 15th century. The stones are very old and names are difficult to identify; however, the good news is, the island has a book shop, and if one wishes to find a Scottish ancestor, this would be the place to go. While we were on the island, I was able to find books that were very helpful and a good read.

On our visit to the cemeteries, we were moved by the graves of unknown soldiers, a poignant reminder of the sacrifices made during the Second World War.

The inscriptions, *'KNOWN ONLY UNTO GOD,'* etched into the stones, appeared to be both British and German and evoked a sense of reverence, highlighting the enduring impact of history on the present. I remained there briefly, thinking about families who would never know what happened to their husbands and sons.

In addition to its natural and historical attractions, Colonsay boasts a welcoming community and a sense of tranquility that is hard to find elsewhere. The islanders we met were friendly and eager to share their knowledge about Colonsay's history and culture, withstand what is sometimes called the wild Atlantic.

Our journey to Colonsay was not just a vacation; it was an opportunity to connect with history and with each other. The island's beauty and rich heritage provided us with a perfect backdrop for lasting memories.

See the Appendix for history.

FROM COLONSAY TO ORONSAY

The island of Oronsay is small and can be reached walking on foot. This island has a peacefulness about it, and the day we visited, I felt a strong need to stay for a while, look around, and think about those men who were committed to spreading Christianity. However, taking my time there almost caused me to be left on the island as the tide came in. My sister was calling me, and we crossed, paddling in shallow sea water. I wish I could go back, but sadly, that is not likely; however, my desire to do further walks and to learn more about history remains.

A NEW ADVENTURE

It was ten years after our visit to Colonsay and Oronsay in Scotland, and at 76, I found myself convalescing from a serious foot injury, bored from being in a wheelchair, vacillating between being angry about an accident that could have been avoided, or being angry with myself for not appreciating how blessed I am. Every day, I would think about people I know who suffered serious illnesses or the result of accidents. I always loved to walk, which is difficult to do in a wheelchair, living in Tennessee in a hilly area. I finally came to recognise that Tennessee is a beautiful place, a place we had chosen to live in after our retirement from a large city. I had only recently retired from a wonderful career that took me to many places in the world, and most of all, I had an exceptional, loving family.

As the months went by, and the monthly visits to my doctor came to an end, I needed to face the facts. I retired, and like many others, found myself needing to adjust to that. The other was to find an interest that I would enjoy and could accomplish. That was hard, too.

I am not a cook or a seamstress or any of those things. I have a sister who has many talents—she paints, she is an exceptional cook, and she writes... She writes, perhaps I can do that. I don't think so; I am a storyteller, not a writer. Then after thinking hard, I knew two things: I love the outside, the wind in my hair, walking our dog, and travelling. I had been to the Scottish Island of Colonsay, and that was one of the special times of my life; I should be thankful.

One day, I was lying in the grass, looking up at the blue sky and feeling so thankful. My grandson came upon me and said, "What are you doing lying in the grass out here in the field?"

I explained this was a habit that I hoped to do for a long time, or until I could no longer get up. Once I could walk again, I began walking around our field, loving every minute.

After walking on Colonsay and many other slightly lengthy walks, including walking around a 15-acre field behind our house, I longed to do more. I do not recall exactly when I first decided to become serious about walking or even considering a very long walk, but my interest in the pursuit of outdoor activities began what some would call 'late in life.'

On my 70th birthday, I decided I would like to start running. Perhaps an odd decision, since I had never been an athletic person. In fact, I was one of those kids who were last to be picked for a game. But in our office, it seemed to me that everyone was doing some type of exercise, and they were having fun, not only participating in their activities, but also talking about it.

David, our son, had participated in many activities during the years he was in college. In fact, he bicycled from Atlanta to Seattle when he was a junior at Georgia Tech. After college, he married and had children, began a career, and with a full life had less time to do what he clearly enjoyed. However, their family enjoyed hiking up Mt. LeConte in Tennessee, with a height of approximately 6,500 feet, which was no easy feat, especially when including three young boys.

In later years, he began trail running, hiking, and participated in numerous running events, and he is still pursuing increasingly exciting events. So, I decided I wanted to run, even though I was the eldest employee in our office. David was very supportive and helped me find the right training.

In November of 2011, I ran in a 5K. I should point out that it was my first and my last. I came in third in the women between 70-74 group. When I was told that, I asked David how many were there in the group—three? But the outdoor activity bug had bitten me. I always loved to walk, coming from England, where walking is a pretty common pastime. My sister and I would sometimes go on

Sunday afternoon walks with our parents. Although I am unsure as to how far we walked, I am pretty sure it wasn't too far, but those times left me with wonderful memories.

As I started walking every day, if I walked a mile, I would push a bit and walk two miles and so on. I recall the day I walked five miles for the first time. I called my husband, Roger, who was out of town.

His response was, "If you keep that up, you will wear your shoes out!!!"

Feeling a little deflated, my stubbornness only caused me to set even higher goals. Walking became much more than distance. In Tennessee, where we now live, there are many wonderful places to walk. Being out early in the morning is as good as it gets. Walking in the moonlight is an experience one cannot explain; it is incredible. I walked in really cold weather, one day in 11°F, over the field behind our home. I loved it. I slowly developed a better understanding of walking. When we are all on a walk, we do not know what lies ahead. I'd like to quote the Danish philosopher, Soren Kierkegaard: "Do not lose your desire to walk. I know of no thought so burdensome that one cannot walk away from it."

Each day, I say a prayer of thanks for the health and strength to walk many miles at my age. I became convinced that I can enjoy this activity for a long time despite having cracked a vertebra in my back, hiking up Diamond Head in Hawaii. I would also be remiss if I didn't say a big thanks to my physical therapist and trainer, Philip Hill, whose skill put me back on my feet, and for his constant encouragement. Along with my cardiologist at St. Thomas Hospital, Dr. Dante Graves, who encouraged me every step of the way.

EARLY SPRING 2016

At that time, I began training in earnest. I found people who had done long walks, read blogs, and watched YouTube videos of walkers and hikers. I was clear about one thing. I wanted to do my walk in England. As a child, I walked the lanes in the Norfolk village I grew up in. I remember so much about those days, wild roses blooming, crabapple trees in full blossom, bees buzzing, and rabbits hopping across the lane. This was a time when children were free to roam.

Elizabeth Gozny, an English poet, said it so well in her poem, *Serenity:*. "Where the wild rose sheds its blossom through the winding country lane. Where the sunshine filters patterns as the day is on the wane."

SUMMER 2016

I plodded through the hot, humid days of a Tennessee summer. Many days, my daughter-in-law, Doris, would accompany me. That was nice because most of my everyday training was on our property here in Tennessee. Once I made the rounds about six times or so, it got boring, so Doris was a welcome companion.

As the summer months passed, I researched more about the area I would be walking in—the shoes, how to keep my feet healthy, and a host of other things. David was invaluable in that he knew the types of shoes I would need, pressed on me to use walking poles, and advised me not to extend my walking too quickly. To quote David, "A marathoner does not run 26 miles for practice."

I bought two pairs of shoes and walking poles. My shoes were purchased with the requirement that they would drain. In other words, waterproof shoes were not the best. I must say the shoes that drained were definitely the best. I walked in lots of mud and experienced heavy rainfall. Not once did I end up with wet squeegee feet.

I initially thought I should walk in East Anglia, probably because I knew this area best. It is the place of my birth and the home of several generations of my family. So, perhaps it was nostalgia that steered me to this area. However, English friends all urged me to consider the Downs in the southern part of England. During my childhood, we had little opportunity to travel much. As a child, I was only once in the southern part of the country on a special trip to see the New Forest.

Roger and I later made a couple of trips to Devon, and I drove down to the coast one weekend after a long week working in London, but that was it. I had discovered a website, www.footrails.co.uk. This company was founded by Alison Howell and co-managed by her husband, David. After numerous emails between Alison and me, obtaining information, visiting David in Bath, where their office is located, and touring the area, I decided my friends were correct; this was a perfect place for my walk.

There were many preparations required, especially accommodation that would be located to fit with my walk. I recognised that David and Alison could provide some of these resources. So, the focus became Southwest England, an area known as Ancient Wessex. Wessex was settled around the 6th century by the Saxons, who, after several hundred years of history, became the reigning dynasty of England. Wessex includes the counties of Dorset, Hampshire, Wiltshire, and Somerset, which constituted the area of my walk. I made sure to include Hampshire.

SEPTEMBER 2016

We arrived in England on Thursday, September 22nd, as planned. It seemed to be a good idea to be there a few days before I started my walk. We had previously stayed at a nice hotel in Windsor; we decided to stay there again for two nights before we went down to the village of Hindon, which is in the county of Wiltshire.

Since we were in Windsor, we toured Windsor Castle before leaving to drive southwest. Following the tour of Windsor, we drove to Salisbury. Salisbury is in the county of Wiltshire, where I will begin my walk. The city is best known for its cathedral. It is also a relatively short distance from Stonehenge.

The cathedral is over 800 years old, Anglican, and is of Gothic architecture, dating back to 1220 when the foundation stone was laid. Construction continued for over 30 years. In and around 1668, the renowned architect and astronomer, Christopher Wren, who was one of the designers of St Paul's Cathedral, visited Salisbury Cathedral. The purpose of the visit was to assess the condition of the building. He then recommended adding strong iron bands inside the spire. The cathedral is beautiful, and for me, the Magna Carta is one of my primary reasons to tour the cathedral. The cathedral has one of only four surviving documents of the Magna Carta, one of the world's most important documents. Although it is now over 800 years old, it remains a powerful symbol of social justice. Many of these rights are adopted globally, including in the USA.

Also, important for me is a statue I had first seen on prior visits, which I was completely overcome by. This statue is a woman who appears to be walking hurriedly away from the cathedral. This time, I found it difficult to leave her, and I asked Roger to take a picture of me holding Madonna's hand. I later learned that the sculptor was Elisabeth Frink. Elisabeth is described as a person committed to the exploration of nature, of suffering and salvation, pain and compassion, terror, and tolerance.

The Walking Madonna walked with a purpose, and it is often pointed out that she is walking away from the cathedral. This is sometimes used as a feminist statement, regarding women's position or lack of, in the church. I held her hand and, after reading more on this statue, learned her hand was worn by the number of people who felt the need to do the same. Women, I would say, felt this need, as I did, in other parts of my working life, and I could truly agree with these statements. In the section on page 135, a poem written by Nicola Slee states well what many women have often felt about hierarchal churches.

We arrived in Hindon, the beginning of my walk, checked into the Lamb Inn, and the next day, drove around to get a better sense of the topography of the area. What we found is a beautiful landscape of rolling hills, which are called chalk downs. It is also a big agricultural area dotted with tiny villages.

Hindon is a larger village than many in the area. The foundation of the village was in the 13th century. Because of size and population, at that time, the village shared a place of worship. However, in 1869, Hindon became a separate parish and the new church a Baptist Church.

The Lamb Inn was delightful and the food very good. We were there two days early, and the next day, we drove into several other villages and found nice pubs that provided good food.

That evening, when returning to Hindon, we heard church bells pealing and asked what the occasion was. It turned out to be bell practice; several bell ringers from other villages attended. My husband, Roger, loves bells, so we walked up the hill to the church where we were invited to climb the steps to the bell tower. We had the joy of sitting in a very small area with six bell ringers listening to the pealing bells. It was a special experience.

BEGINNING MY BIG ADVENTURE

DAY 1: MONDAY

Monday, I had a 4 1/2-mile warm-up walk. It was a delightful day, partly because it was the first, but largely because I ended up walking with a couple and their two young sons. It was not planned this way; they had started out ahead of me. We met them the night before because they were staying at the Lamb Inn, our first stop. The couple's names were Corbin and Meghan. Their sons were almost three and almost six. Edwin was the 'almost six' as he reminded me several times.

They had started their walk earlier because the dad was carrying the little one on his back. I met up with them later and walked with them. It was a joy. Edwin kept me smiling the entire way. Corbin and Meghan were American but had lived in England for over seven years. Both children were born in the UK.

Although they lived in London, they enjoyed the countryside. This was evident since Edwin had walked 4 miles the day before, and on that day, he was walking 4 1/2 miles and still had enough energy to go back and play on the swings in the children's playground. I noticed this on my return as I descended back into the village, impressive for little legs. Between pointing out to me the difference between sheep, cow, and horse poop, Edwin stopped at every place he saw a slug, as they were out everywhere after a rainy day. Loving children as we do, an hour of my first day was a joy with this couple and their sons.

DAY 2: TUESDAY

FABLES OF OLD ENGLAND

My first real walk day started at the Lamb Inn. This was a 9-11-mile walk; I did 10. I walked to the bottom of the road where I had left Corbin and his family at the playground the day before. From there, I walked up the paved hill to a place where a grassy track turned off to the right.

Along the track, I came upon a man leaning against the fence, watching his two dogs bounding through a field of sugar beets. It brought to mind a poem I learned in school, by Walter de la Mare: "What is this life if full of care we have no time to stand and stare."

I hope I will have a lot of time to stand and stare. This track subsequently brought me to a field. My instructions directed me to stand with my back to the fence, look forward '12:00 pm,' and walk in the 10:00 direction. It said a track is clear for you (i.e. Public Right of Way).

Well, it probably was during the spring and summer when it was a huge field of wheat, but the combine had done its job, and it was a field of wheat stubble. However, I had no problem finding a 'wide gap between two sections of the hedge.' The comment about the only bush in the gap was a bit difficult, but I managed to get back on target. From there, I walked across another huge wheat field, going up to the highest point (by the way, Roger estimated these fields were 250 acres and up).

I was to continue down the field to walk along an edge to the left corner. There was a small wooden gate (open) and, per my directions, we walked on to a 'disused road.' It was exactly that, an old tar and gravel surface that was broken up, and through about 20 feet of trees, the 'new' road could be seen and heard.

I soon encountered my first opposition when a woman appeared, walking towards me. She announced I was on her property, in a voice indicative of upper-class English. To say this was unpleasant is an understatement. I gave her plenty of latitude to vent and eventually went on my way. From there, I crossed the road to another track that eventually brought me to descend onto a road leading to a small village. I will note that these roads are dangerous for hikers, very narrow with no sidewalk or shoulder to walk on. I came across the road, into the woods, and onto a trail.

Walking through the woods towards the village was interesting. There had been some rain over a couple of days, and the trail through the woods was very wet—so much so that I walked up on a bank thinking it would be better, especially since I saw a large puddle ahead, about 8-10 feet long. I walked along the bank until I saw ahead that the bank came down a short distance from where the puddle ended.

At the same time, I heard a noise, and two beautiful golden retriever dogs ran through the water, splashing mud everywhere. A couple in Wellington boots came behind them and asked if the dogs had thrown mud on me. I told them I was fine and remarked on what great dogs they were. This couple told me they walked through these woods with the dogs every week or so, but it was wetter than expected that day. They lived in the village and said the dogs would need a shower when they arrived home. I walked to the village with this very nice couple.

The village was East Knoyle, known for a 'famous son,' Sir Christopher Wren, who is best known as the architect of St. Paul's Cathedral. Christopher was born in East Knoyle in 1628; his father was the rector of St Mary's church in the village for many years before moving to Windsor. Christopher Wren Sr. was also a very talented man and produced many plaster designs in the church during his time there. As is my plan, to stop at each village church, I did so at St. Mary's, where I said a prayer for the church and for my walk to be safe and productive. Although East Knoyle is a small village, with a population of only 600, it also boasts a pub called the Fox and Hounds.

If you ever find yourself in the region, I recommend this pub; the food is very good. I met Roger there, and we had a leisurely lunch before I went on my way. Roger and I had stopped in the village shop, and I was amused and delighted to learn that the shop was owned by the village. I assumed that anyone who wishes can volunteer to work in the shop.

As we waited to pay for our purchase, we chatted with a retired Anglican rector, with her white collar. This rector was working in the shop and having a very difficult time with the cash register. So, we waited until another villager came to straighten it out.

Having said goodbye to Roger, I started on my way through the village to the next trail, a car pulled up, and the driver was the rector we had just seen. She asked if I would like a ride.

I said, "No, thank you. I am on a walk.

"Well," she said, "no one will know if you ride a bit."

I answered, "Well, I will."

She smiled and continued her way. Little did I know that before the day was out, I would, in fact, accept a half-mile ride back to the Lamb Inn. I walked through the rest of the village, crossed the road, and looked for the trail. It was supposed to have a gate on the right. Not being able to find this gate, I walked along the road and asked a man who was just pulling into his own driveway. He told me there was a gate, and the ostriches he raised were on the other side of the fence from the trail. I walked back again and realised I had ignored the small gate that was, since it was not on the right as indicated, and it was clearly very overgrown on the other side of the gate.

Nevertheless, I pushed through the gate and found myself in a totally overgrown area. I pushed forward among stinging nettles that were well over my head and blackberry vines all around. Also, roots had grown along what was supposed to be the path. In addition, a fence of barbed wire had fallen into the blackberry vines, and as I tried pushing the vines away, I was scraped by the barbed wire.

After several yards and seeing no opening further up, I decided to try something else. I reversed and arrived back at the gate, where I heard voices. Outside the gate was a woman with a lovely spaniel dog. I must have looked rather pitiful; my hair had caught on the vines, and my arm was bleeding from the wire.

This woman told me she lived in the village and was checking this trail on which she walked her dog in the spring. She had walked over to see the condition of the trail and agreed this was not currently passable. So, she offered to walk back to the village with me and gave me directions back to Hindon.

The road sign said Hindon 5 miles, and though walking on the road was not my choice, not knowing another route, I set out walking on  the road. The app on my phone gave me the distance, so I checked this after a few miles. Since I was a bit concerned about not seeing the village, I was enjoying looking at the scenery ahead and thought I may have missed a turn. The rolling hills, a patchwork of green, yellow and brown, were stunning, but at 5.2 miles on my app, I was concerned there was something wrong; the village and the church spire should surely be visible. That is when I decided to flag down the next vehicle. I was very fortunate, as along came a Land Rover, which stopped. (This is England.)

I asked the driver if I was on the right road to Hindon, and he assured me I was OK. However, he suggested I hop in, and he would drive me there since that was his destination. In fact, he was on his way to the Lamb Inn for his early evening beer. It was only ½ mile, so I didn't feel too bad, and my driver, whose name was Adam, was delightful. He told me about his job as a gamekeeper for Fonthill Estate. His job was to assist guests who came on a hunting trip. He said many were Americans. The day ended with a nice dinner at the Lamb Inn.

DAY 3: WEDNESDAY

LAKES, FOLLIES, AND STONES

Wednesday was to be an 11-mile walk. It was also the day Roger would need to move our luggage to the next inn, which was to be the Compasses Inn in the village of Chicksgrove. To get to my starting trail today, Roger was to drop me off. This trail took me through the entrance to Fonthill Estate. Roger walked a short distance with me; it was a driveway and was paved. Like many of these Stately Homes and properties, they had a long and sometimes rather colourful history.

Today, this estate is the home of Lord Margadale, who I am told is the 20th in line for the throne. I am sure he isn't 'holding his breath.' But the estate is beautiful, very large, probably some thousands of acres.

After Roger left, I took a trail that led me through a field of sheep. This was the second field of sheep I had encountered, and it appeared to me then that sheep have a leader. It was also clear that sheep do not stray from their 'home.' Even if they have no fence, they remain where they should be.

On the left, as I walked, there was a lake and a very old boathouse. In the late 1800s, the stately country homes tended to host many events. I envisioned men and women dressed in the fashion of the day, white pants, striped blazers, and boaters for men, and women in large hats and dresses. In his books about England, Bill Bryson often commented on the 'uniform,' the appropriate dress, which was worn regardless of the weather. I crossed the weir and then reversed my walk back toward the trail.

This took me towards the village of Fonthill Gifford. This is a small village, but it boasts a very nice pub called the Beckford Arms. Roger and I dined there the second night we were in the area, and on another day, had a very nice lunch outside in the sun. Passing the Beckford Arms, my directions led me to the village church, but it was very unclear as to how one got to the church from the road. I was to turn into a driveway that took me to the church, but there appeared to be no entrance to the church, only a high stone wall.

I knocked on the door of a lovely, listed house. The lady who responded to my knock was initially quite terse, telling me walkers often come to her door, and it appeared that maps were frequently wrong. (I later learned she was correct.) However, she then became very friendly and asked me all about my walk and where I was from. She chatted so much that I had a difficult time moving on, so I did not have the time to make my 'church stop.' I finally got on my trail and continued.

The trail took me to some woods, and as I walked, it ascended slowly until I came to a ridge. I was enjoying the walk so much that I did not check to see how far I had come. As I proceeded, the trail began a slow descent, which picked up to become steeper. I noted that my directions for the day gave caution regarding this part of the trail that was very rocky and began to descend quickly. Because this was a forested area, it was dark, and water was seeping through the rocks towards the bottom of the hill. It was necessary to be cautious and to apply 'Philip's Rule'—stay with the committed leg until you have a good, stable place to move forward.

There is no question this 'rule' saved me from a fall more than once. The rocks were very slippery, and some were quite large; in addition, the trail was very narrow. At one point, I slipped and spun a bit and landed on the rather steep bank of the trail. The only result was a muddy and wet bottom—no problem, better than an injury. Finally, I got to the bottom of this trail, only to find it exited to a road and on a corner, making it difficult to determine whether cars were coming. I finally felt safe enough to rush across the road and followed my directions, which were to take a left turn over a bridge. It was a very old and pretty bridge, and a bubbling stream flowed beneath it.

Having made a good, long trek from my last stop, I took this time for my daily meditation. I simply leaned over the bridge and watched the water slowly splash along. It is sometimes difficult to tear oneself away from such a tranquil place to proceed walking again, but I checked my directions and realised I was within a mile of our next accommodation. According to my map, I was to come to a railroad underpass. I kept walking, neither seeing nor hearing anything that might suggest a train. Finally, I came to the underpass and continued just as a fast train went through, shattering the peacefulness of this place. About another ½ mile, and I was in front of the Compasses Inn.

The Compasses Inn and Chicksgrove are worthy of note. Chicksgrove is a hamlet. In the hierarchy of settlements, based upon population, a hamlet is the smallest. My guess is that this village may have had no more than 100 people living there. The inn is a 14th-century public house that was used by travellers and traders who had taken this route since the 12th century. The inn is made up of the original house and a second building, I would guess to be 150 years old.

Roger and I had a room in the original thatched building that had huge beams and beautiful original floors. As with all of the inns Foot Trails recommended for us, this was a delightful place, but our room was just above the pub below, which is very popular but also noisy. So, should anyone wish to make a reservation there and seek a quiet room, it is best to inform the owners.

Although I had completed my fully planned walk for the day, I was not ready to stop. Roger was already at the inn, but was relaxing and watching TV, so after letting him know I was there, I took a walk around the hamlet. It was tiny, and there were few dwellings, but I learned a lot. Chicksgrove and neighbouring Chilmark, another hamlet, are famous for the stone that has been quarried since the 12th century. The quarries date back to the Jurassic period, and the stone is highly sought after for the restoration of listed buildings, among which are Salisbury Cathedral and Hampton Court Palace. The stone itself is now listed for preservation.

I was also somewhat surprised to find no church, but learned that nearby Chilmark was believed to have had a church in the 12th century. There is no visible evidence of that. I continued to walk around until I decided I was ready for a shower and dinner. I had walked about 13 miles and felt great, not only with the terrain and sights but with the challenges and the surroundings.

Another portion of an Elizabeth Gozny poem, "We may not have jewels or riches untold but when there is so much to see. When there is so much that nature unfolds, we are lucky to view it for free!"

DAY 4: THURSDAY

THE KNIGHTS CASTLE

Today was a 5–8-mile walk called 'Knights Castle.' The trail began in the village of Antsy. Roger dropped me off in the village. The first thing I noticed was a village of cottages, probably built in the 1600s, along the road that wound through it, ascending to the end. The next thing was a van parked in front of a 16th-century thatched cottage. The van's company signs said their business was fibre optic service and installation. The driver of the van was in an opening on the road, obviously doing repairs. The oddity of this work taking place in a village of cottages was an indication of how, while English villages have changed, in places like this, the modern blends with the old.

My map directed I was to locate a right turn to a trail on the right side of the road 'just before a cottage.' There were perhaps 12 cottages in the village, maybe more. It was uphill, and I walked through the village, finding nothing as described. I reversed and came upon a lady with two young men; she introduced them as her grandsons visiting from London. The lady told me she had lived in the village since 1990 and did not know any such pathway as I described. But the young men Googled and found a road on the left. They suggested I walk along and take that route.

I walked up to where this road turned, but decided to ask a man I saw sitting in his garden. I called over the gate, and he stood up and gingerly walked (with some difficulty) to the gate. He agreed the directions given by the young men were correct. He told me he walked that trail many times. I asked about his back; he said he had recently had surgery. I told him I had cracked a vertebra in my back the summer before; he was surprised to see me taking a long walk. He said I was an inspiration to him; he had begun to think he would not walk the trails again. I was glad I stopped.

I crossed and went down the road as directed. It was a farm road, of which there are many in this area of the country. It was clear as I walked, I was back on track. The road led me to a stile, my first on this walk. It was quite a challenge because it was high; it did not have a lower step. I wished afterwards I had taken a picture. After looking it over, I took off my backpack, threw my jacket over the stile, along with my maps, and finally figured out how I could get myself on the step and over. I did it; it was quite an ordeal, but I felt very good about it for several minutes as I walked on.

A walk through the woods led me to a road that I followed for two or more miles to reach Wardour Castle ruins. I was supposed to meet Roger there, but my delay in Antsy made me late. There was no cell signal until I reached the castle ruins. I called Roger, and he came and met me. We found a pub and had a late lunch. At that point, I had walked about 6.5 miles according to the app on my phone. I think I had covered the ground in Antsy a couple of times. We then drove back to the Compasses Inn, but I was short on miles for the day and wanted to do more. I found a large field near the inn. This field had a gate with a sign that asked walkers to control their dogs, so it was clearly open for walkers. I walked around the entire field, which was very large, walking along the periphery all the way. It was largely pasture, with a farmhouse visible on the other side, and very hilly.

As I walked towards the farmhouse, I waved to the farmer, who, along with his wife, was outside working. It was a very pleasant evening, mild temperature, not much sun, but the kind of day that was very peaceful. I enjoyed my additional walk.

DAY 5: FRIDAY,

OUT ON THE CHASE

Today's trail started in a village called Swallowcliffe, another interesting name, believed to be Saxon and meaning *slope*. Roger checked us out of the Compasses Inn, where we enjoyed a good dinner and breakfast. Roger drove us to the Royal Inn in Swallowcliffe, where I started an 11-mile walk.

As with most villages, Swallowcliffe has a church—this one, named St Peter's, is a Norman church built in 1842-1843. It is believed it is the second church to be built there since some stones used for the building were thought to have been part of another building. The village has much to see and learn for those who enjoy history. Its charter dates from 940 AD. There were chalk outcrops there, as with much of the area I walked through.

Roger left for the village of Tollard Royal to check us into Perry Cottage. I began my walk, expecting it to be at least 6 miles or as much as 11 miles.

I picked up my trail, and it quickly became clear this walk was going to be in sharp contrast to the previous day's walks. I noticed immediately that the hills were higher. This was an area of chalk downs, and it had become one of my favourite days. Even though there were some strenuous climbs, I had time to go slowly and savour the opportunity. Perhaps I should have been less concerned with finding my way in previous days. I hoped I was getting more experienced.

No matter which, as I climbed, the views were wonderful. I came to the first gate into a field, where more sheep were gently grazing on the lush green grass—*how the cattle in our local area in Tennessee would love this*. I took my time, stopping frequently to enjoy the day. As with the last few days, the weather had been damp, but at the right temperature. There was rain, which could make some of the steeper trails a problem. My first walk took me onto the A30. Unlike some of the small country roads, most A roads are fine. As I have said, I do my best to avoid small country roads that are narrow or have no place to get off while a car goes by. I consider these roads to be avoided, although that may not always be possible.

On these trails, I had two stiles to get over. Typically, fine unless you find one that is broken, and it does happen. Along the trail is a stopping place, about 6 miles in a village named Berwick St. John, where there is an Inn named The Talbot Inn. I had enough to keep going after a good breakfast, but it appeared to be very nice.

Later, I asked for directions to Alvediston to visit the cemetery of St Mary's church. This is the resting place of Sir Anthony Eden and, later, his wife, Clarissa. Anthony Eden became Prime Minister in 1955. At that time, I was 15, and our family, all conservatives, was watching as Prime Minister Eden was sworn in. In later years, he resigned his position due to poor health. During that time in my life, I was just beginning to learn about politics. However, as I was checking to determine the distance to Alvediston, I knew it was too late for this added walk. I hope to go back.

The rest of my day was to be a continuation of interesting places and great walking. I passed a farmhouse and cottages, crossed a field, and entered back on the trail. At this point, the rain began to get heavier. I was now in a field. I walked up a hill towards a place where, according to my map, there was to be a gate. I thought I must have turned incorrectly; I found a small gate that went nowhere. This area was so overgrown that it was impossible to see. Speaking of seeing, I was up a slight hill. The wind picked up, and the rain came down in waves. I could barely see, and there was no shelter. I did what walkers hate to do: retrace their steps. So, I decided to go back to the Manor Farm.

I knocked on the door several times, but there was no answer. I then went down a pathway to the farm cottages and knocked on the door of the first one, but no answer. Suddenly, a woman appeared from the side of the house. She asked me if I needed help, and I explained I had lost my trail. She invited me in. I felt bad since I was dripping water from the peak of my hat and from my muddy shoes. We walked into her warm, cosy kitchen, and she offered me a cup of hot, sweet tea. She explained she had only lived there for a short time and was not familiar with the area. I told her I needed to contact my husband, whom I was supposed to meet at the Talbot Inn for lunch. I had been unable to get any contact, not even a text. I assumed this was caused by the heavy rain.

This special person, whose name I learned was Sarah, said she would be happy to drive me to the Talbot Inn in Berwick St John, since it was a short distance. We arrived there about 2:00 p.m., and the pub was preparing to close for lunch. But when the manager saw how wet I was, she quickly offered hot soup and tea. It was wonderful. Sarah stayed, and we talked. I do not want to invade her privacy, but I felt God had led me to her, and she felt the same way. At that time, we both needed each other.

Many years passed by. We went back to England to see family and managed to meet up with Sarah again. Today, I stay abreast of her life on Facebook. She is an outstanding artist, and I enjoy seeing her success.

DAY 6: SATURDAY

We had a very nice English breakfast at Perry Cottage, ready for today, a rest day, which I would have preferred to be another walking day. However, I decided to heed advice, to plan an outing together, which would be good for both of us. We looked at places we might spend the day and selected Avebury.

Avebury is an ancient village with evidence of farming activities going back almost 6000 years. Today, a very nice village has grown up there. But most importantly, this is a World Heritage Site, home of the largest stone circle in the world. Like many, we had twice visited Stonehenge in the past years, so we were surprised to find that 25 miles from there was a much larger stone formation.

Roger and I walked through the massive stones and took pictures just to show friends how different these stones were. I must say that if travellers are seeking to see Stonehenge, they should also see Avebury.

Avebury boasts a number of historic buildings, the Avebury Manor and St. James Church being only a portion of the antiquity. The oldest part of the church is Anglo-Saxon, stone, built in the 9th century. It is thought that it replaced an older building constructed with wood and mud. Throughout the centuries, the church has had additions and replacements based on research and other means. It appears that Avebury was a part of ancient ceremonial sites and, with other henges in this part of England, created a vast sacred landscape.

That day, the village was holding a garden fete, a truly English tradition and something I had not participated in for many, many, years. The highlight for me was the ferret race. I loved watching this little animal race and holding a small ferret. Village fetes have many activities, fancy dress, baby shows, dog shows, and so much more. This is usually a fundraiser for the village church.

There is so much to see, both in the village and the surrounding stones. After walking for an hour or more, we had a nice lunch in an old pub in the village.

Another highlight was to drive to Shaftsbury, a town that dates to the 1500s, and being one of the highest towns in England (750 feet), it provides great views, historic buildings, and cobble streets. The most famous and very steep, being Gold Hill.

St. Peter's Church is at the top of Gold Hill and is the oldest church in the town, dating back to the 1400s, but could be earlier. The church has a very unusual past, having been made redundant but once again rising to be a beautiful, light, and bright church. The Half Moon restaurant was comfortably cosy, and the food was good. While the visit to Shaftsbury was pleasant, I was happy to get back to my routine. We took the A30 back to Tollard Royal, taking our time to see the countryside and enjoy the area.

DAY 7: SUNDAY

Today, we checked out of Perry Cottage, and Roger moved us to The Inn at Cranborne. My walk was relatively long, but I was looking forward to that. I could start the trail in Sixpenny Handley, but I preferred to take the trail from my map, extending my walk from 8.5 miles to 12 miles. Sixpenny Handley, one of the larger villages and one that is much more 'modern,' was largely rebuilt in the 1800s after a fire. Roger met me in Sixpenny Handley so that we could see the church together. After that, he went to the village of Cranbourne to check into our next accommodation.

The church in Sixpenny Handley is a 14th-century church of England. However, history is rather difficult to follow. As with some other churches, there are parts going back to other points in history. The chancel and nave date back to 1359. There is much to see, and I enjoyed seeing the font, which is believed to date back to 1277-1280. It was moved from another part of the church to the more traditional area under the tower. It is a beautiful piece of stonework and a part of the church that I always enjoy. Another interesting part of the church is the churchyard.

After asking questions, I learned that this is the result of a plan/organisation called the Living Church Project. This project is said now to cover over 600 churches. I had seen such activity in other churchyards, but assumed they were behind with their mowing. However, the idea is to save sacred ecosystems, limiting mowing to one time each year, which is the way churchyards would have been a long time ago. No pesticides are allowed, and now this place is a haven for birds, butterflies, etc. It was a nice, tranquil place.

Before Roger left, we had stopped in the Sixpenny Handley village store. We seem to have taken a liking to these places; they are local and give one an opportunity to meet local people. Also, they offer local produce, which includes Dorset apples, which are yellow and sweet. I enjoyed these when I was walking.

I needed to move on. Following my map for over two miles, I saw a farm and walked across fields towards the town of Farnham. Being Sunday, there were limited places to get a snack, but I learned there was more history. Like so many English countrysides, Romans, Normans, and others settled these places, becoming a pottery centre. They left more behind, since large amounts of Roman coinage have been found near Farnham. Today, Farnham is supported by railroads and roads. The town had a museum, but I didn't stop as it was Sunday. I saw the church nearby, St Peter's, and although it was open 24 hours, I continued. This was an area of vast lands for hunting and beautiful countryside.

Sitting in the grass to rest, I could smell the freshness and thanked God for the opportunity that I must explore. Surprisingly, I saw a few animals, but pheasants were all around. I saw one plantation, but understood there were more. The trails were good, easy walking, although occasionally uphill. I knew I had to continue to get to Cranborne, where I would join up with Roger at the Cranborne Inn. Tomorrow, there was still more to see and enjoy in this area.

We had an unexpected visitor the other evening, Saturday. David Howell of Footrails. He was in the area, doing his job of checking out the Inns they recommended to their walking clients. I think he was a bit worried about me as for the first time, I made a call to their office, having come to a place where my directions were very confusing, in fact, impossible (this was the first and last call I made to their office).

We had a long talk about walking in general. It was then I realised most of Footrails' clients walk in a group, either guided or unguided, or perhaps just a couple. I would have disliked that intensely. David talked about how he and Alison checked out the trails. He said it was always better to have two people when one came to a confusing place or juncture. The decision between the two was likely to be better.

I could understand that, but I preferred being alone; it was just part of the experience. My focus was to do a better job of reading maps. But my experience of retaining help was to discuss clearly what my expectations are. When we first met David and Alison, I told them I planned to walk alone and to walk 100 miles. I think they felt I was unaware of how problematic this could be. Certainly, I had never had this type of experience before, and I was 76!!!

Part of my plan was to experience something I had never done before and find out how adventurous I could be. I saw no danger. I had a phone, good shoes, snacks, and water. Following that discussion, I decided I would get my assistance, if needed, from the folks I met. Many of them knew trails that were close to them. Having said that, the selection of accommodation was very good, something we clearly needed help with.

I then continued to the village of Pentridge, another very ancient village. Pentridge is translated as '*The Hill of the Wild Boar*.' This area is situated at the edge of 'The Chase,' where I had walked the day before. Feeling that it was my best day so far, today was just as perfect. The village is located among Neolithic, Roman, and Saxon earthworks. I remained, like most of us, in awe of the amount of work it must have taken to move so much of the earth, which was visible in many places in the area. Of interest nearby was the Brokerly Dyke, which, it was said, had been dug, probably as a defense to keep out Saxon invaders. The village is also the home of St. Rumbold Church. St. Rumwold, possibly named Rumbold at the time of his birth, is said to have been born on the first day of November in the year 662. Knowing the date alone is amazing, but wait until I tell you the rest of the story.

Immediately after his birth, Rumbold said, "I am a Christian." He was said to be baptised on the third day (at his insistence), and after reciting a confession of faith, he died. Per his request, his remains were moved many times. Today, there exists only a plaque to the infant St. Rumbold at the University of Birmingham. But I digress. The best part of this walk is the Pentridge Hill, which is said to have been formed by a more resistant chalk band. I walked through the village of Pentridge, a nice little village that probably had no more than 250 inhabitants.

Earlier, as I was walking into the outskirts of the village, I met a woman, possibly in her 50s, with a man in his 80s. It appeared it was her father, whom she was visiting, and taking him for a walk, a very slow walk, to see his beloved countryside. I walked slowly with them, and he told me he had lived there all his life, except for the war years (WW2). I left them on their walk and proceeded on a road that came to a farm.

Since my directions indicated I should go through the farm, past buildings, it did not seem to be correct. I saw no one to ask, but decided to turn around and go back (sometimes, a big mistake). I walked out of the farmyard and saw a road that appeared to go some distance to a hill ahead. I knew that was the right way and continued. It was a beautiful day. The sun was shining, and it was about 65 °F. No humidity and a light wind. The hill was about 600 feet, and upon reaching the upper level, it provided two routes, one straight to the top, the other circling around and up. I took the latter because I wanted to see the views from all sides. I stopped to rest near the top and lay in the grass, with the wind blowing slightly in the long grass with a lovely fresh smell. I sat up and looked down at the surrounding countryside.

As is often the case, I would have liked to have stayed longer. But I continued up until I came to a ridge from which one could see from both sides. This ridge walk was open at first, then turned into a woody terrain. I would say it was about a two-mile walk along the ridge. And I enjoyed every minute, stopping occasionally to look at each side until only one side was visible to my left. The route I can go brings me back to the village of Cranbourne. This was the afternoon I had an experience that, for a short while, took away my feeling of complete fearlessness. First was a man walking towards me about halfway along. What seemed odd and made me a little concerned was that he didn't have a dog or a backpack.

It seems silly to feel concerned about that, but most people I met at least had a dog. I saw him several feet ahead, and I continued to keep my pace. He also continued towards me.

As he reached me, he said, "Nice day," and continued. I felt rather foolish as he went along his way. A mile later, I was to turn onto a trail downward to the village below. I was checking to be sure when I heard footsteps. He was a tall man. Also, no dog or backpack. He was walking at a very fast pace. He walked past me as though we were in a race. Obviously, this was the place that was frequented by local walkers. If I lived there, I would be among them; my anxiety was groundless. It was the only time I had those feelings in all the days I had walked. I continued to walk down until I came to the village of Cranbourne. The last census said the village had a population of about 770.

This village had a long history, having been formed during the Saxon period. The church was formed as a monastery in 980 and remained a priory for many years. The church was named St. Mary and St. Bartholomew. It is a 12th-century building, which was added to in the 14th and 15th centuries. There is a very tall tower believed to be 14th century and a beautiful oak pulpit that is dated 15th century. As I walked into the village, I passed the church I had visited before. I entered an area that looked like the middle of the village with two shops. I walked around the corner and saw the Cranbourne Inn up the hill at the end of the road. I was tired as I climbed the hill; it had been a very long but satisfying day. Roger and I had dinner at the inn, which was a very comfortable place, had a delightful staff, and was a historic place with all amenities. The manager was a youngish woman who was delightful. We were there for three nights. It was a good location, being close to my walking trails.

DAY 8: MONDAY

DORSET CIRCLES

Today, I began from the inn at Cranborne. It was suggested I buy supplies in the village since there was little along the trail I was taking. I began walking from the inn and retraced my steps from the night before, walking back through the churchyard. Today's walk was estimated at 12.5 miles. The weather was nice once again; we were fortunate. After leaving the village, I was on a new route going over fields and farm trails. This was an area known for earth movements, Roman roads, footpaths, and bridle trails.

My directions warned that there were no toilet facilities today, and it was wise to purchase supplies from the shop in Cranbourne. I bought apples, water, and two energy bars. We had a big English breakfast at the inn, and that was more than enough.

Speaking of breakfast, an English breakfast is quite unlike breakfast in the US. It is very hearty and can include several foods, such as the typical  fried eggs, sausage, and bacon, but add to that baked beans, grilled tomatoes, and mushrooms. Delicious!!!

The walk was again going to be different. It seemed that we had left the lovely hills behind and were more agricultural. At one point, there was a small river and a bridge next to a ford, which was a little different. The waterway was called the River Crane and was named after cranes that frequented this river. After several trails and fields, I walked through some woods, exiting to a grassy track that provided some views, close to a place known as 'Wyke Down.' Wyke Down has a gate that takes one to a Roman road that runs to Old Sarum. It was a reminder of how close we were to this ancient settlement. Also, as noted earlier, this settlement and other places, such as Stonehenge and Alveston, are the centre of such settlements.

After leaving the area, I walked some long trails, coming, at one point, to a hamlet named Monkton, up Wimborne. It has always interested me that villages and hamlets are frequently named upper or lower. I'm not sure why they are so called. In this hamlet, there was an example of some very old farm buildings of Manor Farm. There was also a string of villages called Gussages. I understand this Saxon word means *'the place where the stream dries up.'*

My walk took me through Wimborne and past the Drovers Inn. At that time, this inn was closed but had recently been 'saved' by people in the community and was expected to be open soon. Nearby were the ruins of the Knowlton church, inside a henge and earth rings. I was reminded that this area through which I was walking had been settled since 300 BC.

Wimborne St Giles is another village in this group. This village rested within old hunting grounds and is part of the estate of Anthony Ashley-Cooper, the 1st Earl of Shaftesbury. As is the case in so many of these agricultural villages, the people tend to commute to towns nearby.

As with surrounding areas, Cranbourne Chase sits on a large expanse of The Chase and Wiltshire Downs, a chalk plateau. The area provided beautiful overviews, woodlands, and occasionally, a more strenuous walk. But it was worthwhile seeing the farms and villages. My first walk began with a lane leading to a field. It was easy and pleasant. I met at least two people along the way, walking dogs. I said hello and kept walking. I then came to a gated field, stood on the bottom rung of the gate, and surveyed the field, noting there were about a dozen cattle. Not sure of the breed, perhaps an English Longhorn, creamy colour, with very long horns wrapped around the head. However, I didn't meet anyone who knew about the animals.

As I stood at the gate, I began to wonder if I should cross the field; there were two gates, the one I was standing on, and another about 70 yards across the field.

A kind man walked up with his dog, and I asked if it would be safe to go across the field. He smiled and said, "The cows will move away from you. There is also a bull further down the hill; he has enough girls and will not bother you." Ha!

So I went through the gate, carefully attaching the fastener, and crossed the field, only to find three horses on the other side. I love to watch horses, but they are big animals. However, I walked over as though I wasn't worried, and then I felt a warm breath on the back of my neck. I was getting a bit concerned until I heard a girl's voice. She came to the gate dressed in riding gear and said, "She will not hurt you; she is just making friends".

So, after my 'animal experiences,' the trail picked up again at the end of a lane. Good weather, various wildflowers in hedge rows, great views, and nice people added so much to my day, which then passed quickly. According to my phone, on which I tracked distance, I had walked just over 12 miles that day.

DAY 9: TUESDAY

FRINGE OF THE FOREST

Today, we would continue for one more night at the Cranborne Inn. I began today's trail at Breamore. Roger was dropping me off to begin my day's walk, which I believe was about 12 miles. The starting point was Breamore House. This house was a very large Elizabethan Manor home that was finished in 1538. With such a long history, one could just imagine what this house contained, with art and other gems.

For American readers, especially, Breamore House was used for a portion of the filming of *Pride and Prejudice*, Jane Austen's wonderful novel, which was a BBC television series aired in the US in 1996 on PBS. Breamore is a village in Hampshire. The grounds of the house are sacred, probably because within these grounds is a 1000-year-old Yew tree.

After looking at the large iron gate, we decided a tour would take too long, so we turned to St Mary's church in Fordingbridge, also mentioned in the Domesday Book. Of interest to me, the land was granted by King's College, Cambridge, a place dear to me also. Roger, with his eyes always on bells, was interested to see that as recently as 2005, the church bells were recast and rebuilt by a foundry in England. As an aside, we bought our bell, a late 1800 church bell in Michigan. At that time, we learned that foundries were almost extinct in the US.

St Mary's is thought to have been rebuilt around 1150 by the Normans. Continuing work and additions have been made to the church over hundreds of years. This was a tribute to the villagers and leaders of the day. One thing that may be of interest is a memorial to the last British man killed in a duel. His name was James Alexander Seton. St Mary's is today an active church, with services each week; a choir and communion are also weekly.

Prior to leaving the church, intending to look up at the bell tower, I walked back to the rear. I saw a rack for vestments. I was touched by the recognition that no matter where we may be in the world, if there is an Anglican church, one will see the same vestments. In some way, this was comforting. As I typically stopped to take a few minutes in these churches, we found St Mary's church beautiful.

While not intended, after our church visit, Roger and I had a quick lunch at another wonderful pub. The Rose and Thistle is a 16th-century thatched pub in a nearby village. As with many such places in the area, they served local game, which was exceptional. On this day, however, thunderstorms were in the air.

As we came in, our host said, "We are expecting a thunderstorm, which means our power is likely to go out. So, if you wish to have lunch, please order something quickly."

Our lunch was a hamburger! But it was good, served with all the dressings and a drink. The ambience of this wonderful room, with its huge fireplace and chimney, made it all worthwhile. This pub was originally three thatched houses from the

16th century. After falling into hard times, as with others I have seen, it was saved by a local village group (consortium). I found this pleasing: a strong village, willing to save itself. It was one of those places, cosy and warm, with good English food and conversation with others.

After this lunch, I was ready to go and concerned about getting my miles in. Roger left to drive back to Cranborne. My walk was largely on pathways; I was in 'stile' country now. I climbed over more stiles that day than any other previously. For those who do not know, a 'stile' is a structure that allows people to climb over a fence or some other obstruction. It is common in England to provide pathways, but rarely seen in the US. The ground was wet and, again, some places were overgrown, but it was green and fresh. I stopped for a few minutes to settle my backpack and, for the first time, took a selfie.

I walked on a lane that ended in a small but old stone bridge, over a stream that wound around to a road. The first house I saw was one of the most unbelievable thatched cottages I had ever seen. It was picturesque, the kind you see in paintings. I stood in front of the house and took in the typical front small garden with flowers that appeared to have no plan—they were just there. A truck stood outside this house with a load of gardening tools. I was still standing, mesmerised. To me, this was a true English garden—the kind that I had foolishly attempted to recreate in my garden in Tennessee!

I was so enthralled by this house and garden that I failed to take a picture of it! But the man with the truck, who was the gardener, explained to me that he spent most of his time working on the grounds of this house, which belonged to a person in London. He asked me if I would like to see the back area. I was imagining a field of flowers, but I was wrong. It was an immaculate lawn with a raised area of shrubbery, with more flowers and a round pool with a waterfall. We walked back to the truck. The man let down the tailgate, got two bottles of water from the cab, and we spent at least 30 minutes talking. Sadly, I did not get his name, but it meant a lot to me to talk to a person who could create such a beautiful place. I realised it was getting late, and I had to get back to Cranborne and must assess the shortest way. This was truly the fringe of the forest. A beautiful area with some excellent trails.

A good part of this day's walk was walking on roads. As noted earlier, it was stormy. Although I ran into little rain, the roads were very wet, narrow, and winding. Because of the lack of a shoulder, one cannot get onto grass alongside the road, which would have been safer. I continued my walk back to Cranbourne safely.

During the day, while I was walking, Roger had gone down to meet the firemen at the Fire Department in Cranborne. They welcomed him and showed him their trucks and other equipment. He was so appreciative; Roger had been a volunteer fireman in our home community for several years.

DAY 10: WEDNESDAY

DORSET MILLER

Today's walk was approximately 12 miles. I could shorten that if I went with Roger as he moved us from the inn at Cranborne, which we really enjoyed, to The Stapleton Arms in Buckhorn Weston. However, I preferred to make my own trail. Getting off the trail was probably not a good idea; however, there were so many small lanes.

So, I walked to the village of Marnhull. At that point, I sat on the stile in the sun and enjoyed the quietness. Marnhull, it is said, derives its name from the Old English name for the hill upon which it stands. People lived here going back to the Iron Age, when the River Stour was probably still navigable, making transport across Dorset possible.

There was a church across the road, St Gregory's, built in 1175. The name was originally St George and is located in Marnhull. Interestingly, it is listed as an Episcopal Church. The church building is thought to have started about 1150. Like so many villages, the church became the nucleus to found Marnhull.

Another interesting place in Marnhull is the Easter Garden, built out of Chilmark stone (local). This was the work of a designer named Andy McIndoe, who made a tomb-like garden out of the highly valued and listed stone. It stands among Mediterranean plants to represent the story and landscape of Jesus.

After spending some time in the church, I continued, following my adjusted directions. I turned onto a small road, which then turned into a lane, and from there, it was not too far from the trail, but I avoided the branch that curved toward the river and West Stour.

From time to time, seeing the river, I passed through a gate and came to an old wheelhouse. This took me into a garden and along a pretty woodland path, which I enjoyed. I crossed a busy road to the Ship Inn, where I stopped to rest. I was unsure of the time of the day, but I would have enjoyed a long drink other than water; however, the inn was closed.

I read an article by a biker who clearly had spent good times biking through this area. He spoke of the beauty of the place. Interestingly, he wrote that he had decided to walk that day. I am not a biker, but I agreed the walk would provide more time to take in this place at a slower pace. After what seemed like a long walk, I came to the kissing gates and followed the road. The views were nice, but I was missing the higher hills from a few days ago. However, I closed the gates and followed the road into the village of Buckhorn Weston, and our next accommodation was the Stapleton Arms.

I needed to move on from the church, so I turned onto a small road, which then turned into a lane, and from there, it was not too far from the trail. This route bypasses the trail that curves to West Stour, and from there, the trail continues to Stapleton Arms, where we would be for the night.

I passed through a small village called Fife Head Magdalen. This village lies in what is known as the Blackmore Vale. As noted earlier, the area near the New Forest changes from chalk to clay. Given the name of the village, it is not surprising that the Parish church is named St Mary Magdalene. The church dates to the 14th century. Also, like so many others in England, the royalty and lords bought or owned these properties centuries ago. Later generations now own large estates. However, over the centuries, they built churches and maintained them. Inside the church was a monument created by one more Westminster sculptor, named Sir Henry Cheere. The monument was made on behalf of the family of Sir Samuel Newman.

The trails were a mixture of farmlands and trails through fields and occasional villages. Kington Magna is a small village, and its parish church, which is on high ground, has outstanding views that attract hikers and bikers alike.

It was time to take the best way to the inn; it had been a good walk. Today, using the trail, I would have done 11/12 miles. Having adjusted my walk, I ended up at about 9 miles. After reaching the inn, as has been my daily schedule, I took a shower, then soaked my feet in a good pedicure solution. This and two pairs of shoes and four pairs of socks have been my method.

Now, it was time for dinner. The Stapleton Arms is a traditional North Dorset pub. It was very nice, the food was good, and the staff were pleasant.

DAY 11: THURSDAY

Today was a rest day, and the Stapleton Arms provided us with a little booklet called the Stapleton Arms Pub Walk. This was appreciated, but it was a mirror of yesterday's walk. So, we would do as we often did on a rest day, and that is to ride around and look for places of interest.

A person at the inn suggested Stourhead Gardens. Apparently, these gardens were created by a banker, Henry Hoare. Inspired by European travel, the garden included temples, grottos, and a beautiful lake. The area we were in right now had more farmland, but also trails and great views. Not knowing how friendly busy farmers and their workers would be, we didn't stop to chat. Roger, who grew up on a farm in Illinois, would have loved the opportunity. However, some of these farms date back to Medieval times, with stone buildings, and I am sure, much history, but not much similarity.

There were a couple of family short walks, and we took that opportunity. We enjoyed the drive and relaxation. We later returned to Corton Denham, and we found it an interesting village. One issue I have found, and perhaps mentioned, is the closeness of some villages in certain places.

As an example, this village has a defibrillator in the village telephone box. As we know, these telephones are no longer used. Instead, today, many villages have found unique ways to use them. This village has the good fortune of being in a valley between two escarpments, one very high, the other very steep, probably good for the farms around. During my walk in September, I was told that the 'rich hay' was all cut by the end of August. We ended the day with an excellent dinner at the inn.

DAY 12: FRIDAY

INTO SOMERSET

Today's walk moved us into Somerset, another county. We began the day with a good breakfast, the best way to start on a long walk. Roger would be checking us out of the Stapleton Arms Inn and moving our baggage to The Queens Arms in the village of Corton Denham in the county of Somerset. Somerset has a lot to see, and it would have been interesting if I had time. The walk was long, 21 minutes by car, but over 12 miles for the walker.

This walk promised good things: views, trails that were steep but passable, and the area was characterised by long ridges of hills providing shelter to villages in the valleys below. Today, I began a walk about 41/2 miles. The route took me over the surrounding countryside to the summit of the Beacon. This was the highest point in Somerset with an altitude of 1,703 feet. This high point was Exmoor, a national park that borders two counties, Dorset and Somerset. There was a Country House on top of the Beacon for those who wished to enjoy great views.

The higher part of Exmoor is largely grassland, with woodlands on the lower portion; I made no plans to climb. There was a trail from Buckhorn Stapleton to the Beacon. Although I understood the views were incredible, instead I completed about 7 1/2 miles walking from my area to Corton Denham, where we would be spending the night.

Along the trail was the Half Moon Inn, which serves lunch, but I was carrying apples, chips, and water. My breakfast in the mornings was intended to keep me from needing to have big lunches. I have to say this area was a place that one should plan to stay for at least three or four days. It was wonderful to see Exmoor and see goats, wildflowers, and the views, etc.

I arrived, tired, at the Queens Arms in Corten Denham. Time for a shower and footcare, and then dinner. No matter what people say about British food, we enjoyed great meals at these inns and pubs. Of course, I am happy, as this is the food we ate when I was growing up. I understand today's British food is much better than it was during my childhood.

DAY 13: SATURDAY

A KNIGHTS' QUEST

This walking day is called the Knights' Quest. I left the inn at about 10 am. It was Saturday, and as I love English breakfast, I took my time, then left and took a 4.5-mile walk around South Cadbury. The trail is flat, and the views are great. The weather also continues to be nice. There is a Camelot Inn in South Cadbury, a great place for lunch, I am told. However, after a large breakfast, even after about a 5-mile walk, I did not need lunch. The afternoon was a return walk, approximately 4.5 miles, arriving back at Corten Denham, where we enjoyed a leisurely rest of the day.

DAY 14: SUNDAY

It was Sunday morning. Today's walk was into Sherborn. This was a market town. Typically, not large, these towns supply villages and hamlets all over England. Sherborne has a population of over 9,000, very large compared to villages along the way, which may have only 200 or more people living there. Interestingly, 22.7 % of the population is over 65. As in the US, retired people often seek a smaller community for their retirement years.

Roger intended to come to pick me up, but it being my last day, I wanted to walk. The trail back to Corton Denham was just right for what I expected to be the end; the trails were interesting. Often, there are national trails in these areas, and some are easy. For me, it is all about being outside, looking across the hills, and thinking about how it must have been throughout history. There were years characterised by poverty and a lack of security for many people. Throughout my walk, I have had the opportunity to think back on some of the experiences. I frankly do not recall the name of all the villages; there were so many and not necessarily on the trails. The wonder of villages today and the long history of how they developed, largely due to the Saxon era, is another subject discussed in the latter part of this book.

VILLAGES

On my walk, I went through many villages. While the ages of these villages are very similar, time has passed, and they have grown differently. As an example, some have spent money and time to maintain their history; however, others have done less. In the *Appendix* are four books I either had in my library or purchased for information. These books provide more information from specific places in England.

I came through a rather larger village one day. The primary school was getting out, and mothers were waiting, holding the hand of a child, rocking a baby in a pram, and chatting happily with each other. It was a nice day. I took in the scene and then continued, only to realise I had somehow become uncertain as to where I was.

This village had a small 'river' going through, and my map said to find a bridge and cross to the next point. I followed this, crossed the bridge, and instead of the fields I expected, it was the centre of the village. I backtracked and spoke to the young mother of a little boy about 5 years old. I explained that my directions were misleading. I crossed the bridge, and it didn't come into a lane as indicated.

She smiled and said, "There are two bridges, another about a half mile."

I thanked her, and she quickly asked about my destination, where I was from, etc. I explained about my walk. She was so excited, she asked her friend if her little boy could go home with them. Once she had handled that, she turned to me and asked if I minded if she walked with me.

"Of course," I said. "This will be helpful."

She continued questioning me in a very excited way as we walked briskly to the second bridge, where I assumed I would thank her and go on. However, she seemed to be so happy about this walk that she said she would like to continue to the field.

As we came up to the field, she said, "I will give you my phone number and address in case you need anything. By the way, if you need laundry done, I can help with that also."

I explained that it was not necessary and thanked her for her help. Sadly, I didn't get her name and number. She was kind and happy, and it appeared that this village was a happy place.

However, I learned that villages can be very different and have different personalities. I will describe another village I came through on my journey.

Again, I had come through a field and along a lane that turned into a village. This was not unusual. As I walked along, I noticed it was very quiet, and I think the words that would properly describe it are neat and organised. Along the street was a row of houses, several one-storey red brick, most with fenced, pretty gardens. I was now in sight of what I believed was the village centre. There was a circle road in the middle of a pretty, well-kept, grassy mound with a war memorial in the middle. A linked chain circled the memorial. It was almost identical to the memorial in the village I grew up in.

This village centre was like so many across England, and as frequently as I could, when I was in England for work, I would go to see the church and memorial in my village. I was taught to understand the value of the many lives that were lost in the two World Wars. Since I now needed a rest, there was a nice bench on the grassy mound. I decided to take a 15-minute rest, drink some water, and then continue. As I came around the mound, I saw a woman sitting on the bench. I asked if I could join her. She seemed happy to do that, as did the little dog sitting on her lap. I opened a bottle of water, and we began to chat. She had many questions, but the perception I had was that she was lonely.

This person was probably in her early fifties. When I told her how far I had walked, what I had seen, and the beauty of the area, she seemed amazed. I needed to move on, and since the road went out from the circle in a different direction, I explained where I was going and asked for her help. She seemed excited and said, "You will be walking by my house, and if I can take my dog inside, may I walk a little way with you?"

I had not seen what the other side of the village was like. I felt there must have been a school, families, and people laughing, but where I stood, I saw nothing like that. Nor did I see a church tower, although there must have been a church. I was thinking I may have come into the area outside the main village. She explained her husband worked in a city and caught the train early in the week, returning Thursday night (I should add, this was before working at home, etc., began). Also, she was Canadian, so she probably had no close family. I assumed she had no children because she never mentioned it. So, we walked about half a mile before my map directed a turn into another field. She said, "Thank you." I wanted to hug her, but I felt clear that wouldn't be correct. But my continued walk that afternoon was touched by what I had experienced earlier.

I walked on, thinking about how many people I had met throughout my walk, the difference, and how fortunate I felt having the opportunity to step out and decide to walk 100 miles when most people my age would not think of this. What made us different? These are some of the things we think as we walk through nature's beauty. Away from the news, good or bad.

Certainly, we are all different, but to love wide open spaces and take in clean air is something many look forward to. Not everyone is crazy enough to take on a long walk at 76 years of age. But I encourage you. If you think about it and consider taking a walk or a long driving trip, try not to follow up with thoughts that say, *I cannot do this*. Just respond, "I am going to give it a try."

Of course, this takes planning and preparation. I am not special; I was never athletic as a child. I had a long career that involved significant travel, both within the US and foreign countries. But as with many people, nature beckoned me.

The US is a vast, beautiful country. There is so much to see. Try driving on back roads, then branch out to wider areas. Meet new people and be thankful every day.

DAY 15: MONDAY

This was the sad ending, not just because these two weeks' walk had ended. This was the night before having to check out of our last accommodation. I had returned. I walked up the stairs to our room, took a shower, and treated my feet. We then walked down the stairs that exited outside. We walked in front of the inn to enter the dining room.

By this time, it was dusky but not dark. We had a delightful dinner and talked about it as we left the inn and walked back to the door that took us up to our room. This time it was dark, and lights were directed out from the inn. The walkway had no lighting. Roger and I walked down the steps; I was beside him. Suddenly, my foot went down. It turned out the step on my side was broken, and my foot slammed down approximately 18 inches. The pain from this accident was excruciating, but somehow Roger managed to get me upstairs, and I managed to get through the night.

I am sad to say this, but the small emergency hospital we were told could help had minimal X-ray equipment. In the meantime, Roger called to change our flight back to the US immediately. It was early, and we were able to book a flight at midday. From the village to the airport, taking the rental car back, people could not have been more kind.

The following day, almost immediately upon my return, I was transported to Franklin, Tennessee, to the *Institute of Bone and Joint*, a large orthopedic group. I was immediately seen by a foot specialist, had an MRI, and learned that I had suffered a Lisfranc fracture. I was told this fracture typically results from sudden trauma. This exactly agreed with my accident. Fortunately, I had a great doctor, D. Ronald Derr, who not only took care of me for about five months but also understood the emotional impact. I am so thankful for his care.

I spent three months in a wheelchair. Initially, I was focused on my foot and the upcoming physical therapy, but the sadness of not finishing my walk the way I had expected took its toll. One hundred miles and no injuries until I came to those steps.

The night before we were leaving the inn, I had indicated to Roger that I would love to take another two days to walk, but he was ready to go home.

So, how does one get over this? I was 76 years old; I thought I would never take a long walk again. I had the support of my family, who probably hoped I would never again bring up the subject. But two of our children, who are runners and do some hiking, understood the situation. During the time I was convalescing, my son sent me videos of walks in England, Ireland, and Scotland.

This may not sound good for some, but here I am—*this picture was taken two years later off the coast of Ireland in the Dingle area.* So, don't give up. I have more stories to tell.

Photo of June on a clifftop in Ireland.

SEPTEMBER 2019,
DINGLE, IRELAND

After my accident and recovery, my husband and I took many trips. One would think this was all enough, but I desperately wanted to have another walk, and the years of my life were advancing fast. In 2019, I was 79 years old, which was not of concern for me, but it certainly concerned my family. Then, my youngest daughter, Tammy, stepped in and offered to join me on another walk. We chose Ireland and the Dingle Peninsula.

Although it was our plan to begin hiking right away, it was very evident that one could enjoy a vacation in the town of Dingle. Having settled in a hotel there and returning from hiking each day, we quickly came to understand that the Irish music, friendly people, and of course, nice drinks were a great addition. This was a very different walk from the Downs in England, but it was exciting. However, the big difference was that some places were now too difficult for me than the area in which we started our hiking. We walked in beautiful areas such as Dún

Urhin-Clogher, Dunquin-Coumeenoole, and many more.

The beauty of the wild Atlantic Ocean, the beach, and the cliffs.

Hiking on some rocks and ruts was difficult, and I didn't want another accident. Nevertheless, we had many days of good weather, the beautiful cliff walks, and great evenings. One area we did not see was the Blasket Islands, part of an archipelago of islands. The Blaskets are no longer populated, although it is possible to take a ferry there. People who, like me, find joy in the wind and natural elements, would love to stand on the Great Blasket. There you can watch puffins, sea lions, and the many birds and animals that have made the Blaskets their home. The Great Blasket is only a few miles from the coast and about four miles from the town of Dingle to the Great Blasket Ferry.

This was a very different walk from the Downs in England, but it was exciting. However, the big difference was that some places were now tough for me.

I have often said that walkers and hikers are some of the friendliest people. Hiking along with my Leki poles from years back, some very steep places were tough for me. I encouraged my daughter to continue to hike on the cliff tops. Getting up to those levels requires a strong upper body. As I stood thinking about how I could do that, along came two hikers. One pushed, the other pulled, and I was up there. They introduced themselves as Canadians of Irish descent. They had worked and saved for this vacation. It didn't stop there. They came back to check when I needed to go back down. They later came and helped me down easily. I spent about an hour or more on the cliffs, enjoying the sights and the breeze.

I could see my daughter down on the beach, clearly enjoying the beauty and peacefulness. She was happy having some time from work and her busy schedule. I will always be so thankful that we had this time together, and that I had the chance for another walk. It was a sunny, windy day up on those cliffs, with the waves of the Atlantic Ocean below. I will always remember it.

How far did we walk? I have no idea. In five days or so, we probably walked 55 miles. It was a very special trip. Walking along the high cliff tops was my favourite, and the views were incredible. The Atlantic Ocean is often called 'wild.' I think that is an excellent description.

APPENDIX

HISTORY OF THE ISLANDS

PART I:
Colonsay

This Hebridean Island (Colonsay) was home to people as early as 850 BC. Writings indicate that the population arrived when the climate improved sufficiently to support these people, likely sometime after the last ice age. The stone circles on Lewis Island are 5000 years old. This amazingly predates the stone circles of Stone Henge, Avebury, and other henges. Celts, believed to be a collection of tribes, are thought to have originated in Europe. They may have had similar beliefs and language in common. Celtic traits are often said to be *persistence* and *red hair*. Also, it is said that 46% Irish and 36% Scots are carriers of the red hair gene. (We have a few redheads in our family, and we are also pretty persistent, but we have no Scottish family).

There is some research that suggests these variants are an adaptation to cloudy weather. Even today, the weather in Colonsay changes abruptly. When the air is clear, it is possible to see other islands 10-15 miles away. On certain days with high sun, the Northern Hemisphere is light, and possibly, one may be able to stargaze or see Northern Lights.

While Celts settled much of Scotland between 700-900 AD, the Hebrides were invaded by Vikings; however, it is thought that Colonsay, being a key location southward along trading routes, was not as affected.

Moving forward, about 1687, it was the end of the true monarchy of Scotland and the end of the McDonalds and Catholicism. The next two centuries were a time of rapid agricultural and social improvement, sadly accompanied by the removal of much of the original population. From 1737, there was voluntary emigration to North Carolina. This was interrupted by the American War of Independence. After which came 'The Clearance' between 1790-1860 or so, when people were forcibly removed from the land that had been inhabited for generations. It is estimated that 150,000 Highlanders were cleared from their lands. This was a brutal event, which at the time was further impacted by the potato famine.

For much of the 19th century, conditions were harsh in Colonsay, but they began to improve later due to intervention by the state. Crofters were spread through the islands, which led to the *Crofters Holding Act* in 1886, after disputes between crofters and landlords. This gave crofters tenure. It was some time before further changes, when in 2003, the government introduced the *Land Reform Act*, giving communities the right to purchase and access to Scotland, an action which is now praised.

PART II:
Oronsay, Scotland

The island of Oronsay is close. In fact, one might consider Colonsay and Oronsay as one island. Lord Strathcona owned the island for many years and sold it to Adam Burgus. Actually, the current owner has been part owner for several years. When Mrs Frances Colburn's husband died, she became owner. Mrs Frances is American and visits the island frequently.

The island is low-lying, barren, and rocky, indented, with sea lochs. It can be reached on the beach from Colonsay at low tide, just two miles each way, and full well worth the stroll. It has several historic artefacts, such as the Oronsay Cross, 6th century, depicting the crucified Christ. There are three other crosses, especially a tall Celtic Cross, which is very high and has an inscription of Prior Colin, who died in 1610. There is also a High Cross carved out of solid stone; it is said to be about 121 feet—another one of those things that seems to have been impossible to accomplish at that time.

Importantly, the Augustinian Priory, which is said to be the best-preserved medieval monastery, is on this island. It is known that the priory was in existence in 1353. It was considered a monastery of canons and monks.

In the fifth century, monks made what is believed to be—and certainly must have been—a perilous trip to Ireland. St Columba was a Christian missionary, possibly Celtic. He was born on December 2nd in the year 521 AD. He had been one of those who founded the priory and brought Christianity to Scotland around 563 AD. During his educational period, he was one of 12 students of St Finnian who became known as one of the Twelve Apostles of Ireland. From there, he became a monk and was later ordained as a priest. History asserts that around 560, he was involved in a quarrel with St Finnian, apparently over the ownership of an ancient manuscript. This quarrel ended in open warfare and a large loss of life. There were some who thought St Colombo should be banished from the church. He left Ireland for Scotland, and it is said that this was a self-imposed exile, as penance. Other writers say he intended to win as many to Christ equal to the number who had died in the battle. (Perhaps this was God's plan.)

After his move, he went on to found an abbey and to spread Christianity. Arriving on the white sandy beaches, such as he had walked on, he built his first Celtic church and established a monastic community on the island of Iona, a small island in the Inner Hebrides that continues to value the work of this Christian man.

St Colombo died on Iona on June 8th, 597. Since he was about 42 years old when he left Ireland, it is likely that he was on Iona for over 50 years. Since I have not been to Iona, I have not had the opportunity to see where he lies.

St Colombo not only brought Christianity to Scotland, but he also built monasteries, wrote books, and hymns. He is a Patron Saint of Scotland and one of three Patron Saints of Ireland.

PART III:
Swallowcliffe Village

There has been much research in this area, especially at Swallowcliffe. This work reveals indications of early settlements, suggesting people were there in Mesolithic times. The result of much investigation supports evidence of the presence of farmers, potters, and weavers. In 1966, the Ministry of Public Buildings and Works provided further research that revealed a rare Anglo-Saxon grave. This grave contained many interesting things; one was a casket containing 14 articles that could be identified, such as silver and bronze rings and other objects.

According to my reading, the Domesday Book mentions seven households and land that were taxed! Wilton Abbey held the greater amount, and others, including even unfree tenants, were taxed! The total value was very low, probably in line with other areas. This total value was under £5.

More surprisingly to me, the population was thought to be between 40-60 households, with the current population less than 200. As with other villages in surrounding areas, farming and early textile weaving were a meaningful part of work; in addition, the clay available resulted in making clay pots and other small tools. The village today is a good place to live. The villagers have many events, such as the Swallowcliffe Society, which continues interest in the history as well as the natural history of the area. Like many other villages, the Royal Oak, the village pub, was purchased by a consortium supported by the village.

CHURCHES

It was my intent when I planned a walk in England that as I walked into villages, I would try to spend some time in the village church. I am so happy I made this part of my walk. It was quite surprising that most of the churches were open. Surprising, because so often the churches have beautiful artefacts and relics, and in some cases, very valuable books that must be preserved. These relics are important to determine which group of early settlers developed beliefs and skills to build such beautiful places.

The Celts are believed to be the earliest settlers of the British Isles and would have begun moving long before others. They came from Central Europe and are thought to have shared a wide range of languages and beliefs. However, in recent years, British archaeologists have increasingly questioned whether Celtic society shared languages and religious beliefs. No matter who had the most impact, the slow development over many years gave Britain so much.

Most of the churches I spent time visiting were along my trail. To quietly sit in any church is peaceful, but as I sat in these ancient churches, I thought about what memories there were. In later years, people came to pray for the men who were at war, babies were christened, young people confirmed, and weddings and burials were held. Then, there was Mothering Sunday, Harvest Festivals, and Christmas services, with beautiful carol singing. Even today, most villages have a historic church that provides support and peace.

14th century Baptismal Font

ST MARY THE VIRGIN – EAST KNOYLE, WILTSHIRE

The Parish Church of St Mary the Virgin is a Grade 1 listed building and has been the heart of the parish for over a thousand years. It has Saxon origins and is considered the most significant building in Knoyle. The nave dates from the 13th century and the tower from about 1450. The building started before the 1066 conquest, with the oldest addition being the chancel, pre-Norman. On the property near the church is a Saxon Cross shaft, dated between the 7th and 9th centuries. There is some indication that the cross may be earlier than the church itself.

The great Sir Christopher Wren, the architect of St Paul's Cathedral, was born in a cottage in East Knoyle, probably tiny and poor. His father, also named Christopher Wren and referred to as Dr Wren, was the rector there at that time. They had to leave their home and move from the rectory, due to a fire. Sadly, there are no remains of the cottage; however, the rectory still stands.

ST JAMES – ANTSY PARISH CHURCH, WILTSHIRE

St James was first built in the 13th century, with the nave of the church added about 100 years later. This church can trace its origins to the reign of King Stephen, 1135-1155. It is said that nothing remains of the first church. However, the oldest part of the current church, the chancellery, was built in the 13th century during the reign of King Henry 111 (1216-1272). About 100 years later, the nave was built.

St James is a Grade 11 church, and according to architects, this is largely due to its design, sympathetic alterations, and an unusual nave roof. Evidence of change through history is seen by differing masonry stone, such as a reddish sandstone in the chancel and a lighter stone in the nave. The windows were all replaced at the end of the 19th century.

SHAFTSBURY ST PETER'S DORSET

St Peter's is the oldest church in Shaftesbury, where, in medieval time, there were eleven churches. It was built at the top of Gold Hill as a pilgrim church outside the walls of a Benedictine Abbey. John Schip is the first known incumbent (1305). However, there is evidence of an earlier building on this site, in the form of ancient foundations under the nave floor.

This church has had more than one life. It is a story that has touched me since I first read the history of the church. At the time, a steep cobbled street dominated the town of Shaftesbury. Looking down this street has been described as one of the most romantic views.

History shows evidence of significant poverty during the 14th and 15th centuries. The French-American War (1337-1453), further exacerbated by the Black Death (1346), which depleted the population, seriously impacted the ability of the church to continue. However, the present structure, the lower part of the tower, and other parts of the church were added by the 15th and 16th centuries. This resulted in substantial changes to the building.

In the years following, other churches were established and built, and St Peter's became used only for occasional services until, in 1955, many efforts were made to reestablish the church, and in 1970, friends of St Peter's raised significant funds. Having been made redundant in earlier years, on September 30th, 1977, a service of rededication was performed, making St Peter's the first church in the country to become a full-time parish church after being redundant. This was done with the authority of the Crown.

ST PETER ad VINICULA – ST PETER IN CHAINS – TOLLARD ROYAL, WILTSHIRE

The present building has evidence of its foundation, and its age is also seen in 13th-century windows and the style of the tower arch in the nave, which bears marks of a Gothic style. It appears that this was a church as early as 1215. In 1412, a new bell tower was built. St Peter's continues to be an active church.

ST MARY'S BREAMORE SAXON CHURCH, HAMPSHIRE

This church may have been built on a royal estate, as what was then thought to be a Saxon church. Although today it still has the sense of being part of an estate, the Anglo-Saxon inscription over the South Porticus was written in the reign of King Ethelred. 938-1013. The Saxon doorway, carved with letters that read: 'HER SWUTELATH SEO GECWYDRAEDNES THE,' which loosely translates as "Here is manifested the word to thee."

The church is today considered one of the most important buildings in the south of England. However, as with many of the ancient churches, during periods of change, for example, a change to other beliefs may make an impact.

CORTON DENHAM ST ANDREWS CHURCH, SOMERSET

There has been a church in Corton Denham since the 12th century. However, the new building dates from 1869, when the Norman church was taken down because of its small size and bad state of repair. The original church had, throughout its history, apparently held an important position in the village. Exceptionally stained and painted glass dates back to 1870. These works were done by a painter who was known for his work all over Europe. Also, old relics and other pieces of history are retained, including early photographs of the original church and of the new church after it was completed. The present church is dedicated to St Andrew. Happily, it is now an active church with an excellent website and a YouTube video.

MARNHULL, ST GREGORY, DORSET

St Gregory's church is a Grade I listed church, built around 1250. In and about 1150, Marnhull had no church of its own and was part of another parish. When Salisbury Cathedral was still at Old Sarum, and the writing of Magna Carta was many years away in the future, Marnhull became a separate parish. A small rectangular stone church was built with four arches and an aisle on the north side of the nave. The first rector was appointed in 1250. Importantly, the church continued to grow, and additional building was done.

Another interesting structure is a tomb effigy. According to recent visitors who specialise in medieval tombs, this is one of only six tombs in the country made from Derbyshire alabaster.

The churches listed above were all on my walking trails and in villages. Sitting in an ancient place of worship, as these churches are, is very peaceful. However, it causes one to think about what the walls would say if they could talk. We cannot imagine the historic times, but in the last 100 years, there was much to think about as I sat quietly. There were two world wars. Many of the churches have plaques or outside monuments in memory of lost lives. It is hoped that those who came to church in those years found peace. But then there are joyful times. Christening new babies, confirmation of older children, and wonderful Christmas services.

Most of the historic churches in England are given a grade by the Historic Buildings and Monuments Commission. Grade I being the highest grade, as follows: Grade I buildings that are of exceptional interest. Grade II are listed as particularly important buildings of more than special interest. I understand there are 295 Grade I listed buildings in Wiltshire, the first county in which I began my walk. Clearly, few have time to visit all of them. A Grade I building can be a castle, a cathedral, a memorial, or even a house.

Typically, a Grade 1 or 11 listing in England is old and has a special historical, cultural, or architectural interest. There are, of course, many buildings that receive a listing. The Commission also recognises a building of national importance that has been deemed worthy of protection.

St Gregory, In Marnhull Dorset UK. The original building was 12th century. The new structure was built in 1869.

CHURCH OF ST MARY & ST BARTHOLAMEW, CRANBORNE, DORSET

The Church of St Mary & St Bartholomew was a Saxon Benedictine Monastery, founded in 1102 until it was dissolved in 1540. However, the tower, nave, and aisles from the priory were all saved to form the parish church of Cranborne. The building has a tall tower, possibly 14th century, and several artefacts in the church, including a 12th-century Norman roof, an early Norman doorway, and evidence of funerary practices.

This church has a long history, some of which can be found in the *Domesday Book*. This information states that the Cranborne Abbey was one of the most important monastic foundations in the region, holding some 13,000 acres across several counties. However, as can happen, politics changed the importance when King Henry VIII, around 1540, dissolved the monasteries, resulting in a shift of importance, and St Mary's was reduced to a priory church. However, the main church was rebuilt due to the demolition and was reconsecrated in 1252, being renamed St Mary's and St Bartholmew.

Today, St Mary's church, in its role in the community, is a significant and active place of worship and community involvement.

It may interest readers to know that during the Dissolution of Monasteries, the Cranborne Abbey was sold for £14, 3s 3d.

AVON TYRELL

Being close to the New Forest brings back so many memories for me, and the primary reason I decided this was where I chose to walk. The year would have been 1954 when I was given the opportunity to attend a one-week special event at Avon Tyrell, close to the New Forest, and a minimal drive time to Southampton.

The Manor House was built in 1891. The story behind it is long and interesting and at times humourous. The house was built as a calendar house with 365 windows (days in a year), seven outer doors (days in a week), 52 rooms (weeks in a year), 12 chimneys (months), and four wings (seasons).

This house has had many uses and was used as a convalescent home for injured New Zealand officers in World War One, and then requisitioned by the army during the Second World War as an intelligence gathering post, hospital, and morgue. By 1954, it was given a new role. In 1946, the Manners family, who owned the estate, put the property in trust to be used by 'the Youth of the Nation.' This UK youth organisation is now the custodian.

Why was this important to young people at that time? The Second World War ended in 1943, but so many people had been left damaged in many ways in a terrible war. Children and young people were also affected.

By the time I was of the age to attend a program away from home, I was able to travel to Avon Tyrell. The program I attended included mixing German youth with English youth. It is my opinion that this was an excellent idea. My father served as a Royal Marine Commando from 1939 to 1946, and he supported this program.

I loved the time I was there and remained in contact with a German boy who later became an interpreter at the United Nations. Sadly, as we grew through years of family and children, and work, we lost touch.

BOOKS THAT MAY INTEREST
READERS AND WALKERS

During planning for my walks, I sought books I thought may interest me. This list may not be appealing to some readers. However, I found that each of them provided knowledge, insight, and pleasure.

The Crofter and the Laird was the book that resulted in my selection of Colonsay, in planning a walking opportunity. It was truly full of information, and at that time, my sister and I decided this was a good holiday place. For me, who hoped to walk, it was perfect. But the area surprised me. As noted, I found it hard to believe an island off the coast of Scotland and the sometimes-wild Atlantic Ocean had such beautiful beaches. It was a small island and offered so much. The author, John McPhee, wrote this book in the 1960s. It was valuable to me, and I bought a second copy for my dermatologist, who was interested in taking his sons on a trip to Scotland.

The English Village—History and Traditions. As my walking plans became firm, I knew I would be walking through many villages. I noticed this book and decided to see what it could offer. It was full of good information, but I came to realise that the books' village locations were located north of where I walked and grew up. Nevertheless, it was a good read for me. The author, Mark Wainwright, has written many books.

Wild about Dorset. Because I knew my walk would take me through Dorset, I decided to buy this book. I was not disappointed. The author and I could probably spend a long evening learning more about his love of this place. This book is written like a diary so that a reader can take in the change of seasons. Since I was walking through Dorset in September, I was hoping to read about the flowers or birds, but September was the author's time for butterflies and bats. Nevertheless, I enjoyed his knowledge. The author, Brian Jackman, has travelled widely, as have I. If we were to meet, our conversation would be his home county, the snowdrops of winter, and the return of the birds in Spring.

THE NATIONAL TRUST & THE ENGLISH HERITAGE

Both organisations were founded to protect and promote historic sites and places, importantly to make them accessible for enjoyment and preservation.

As I was walking through villages, I frequently noticed the National Trust's presence, particularly in churches and other historic buildings, many of which are listed as National Trust properties. When we speak of listed buildings, this generally refers to those protected and managed by the National Trust.

THE NATIONAL TRUST

The British National Trust was founded in 1895 as a UK-based charity to promote places of historic interest and natural beauty, ensuring they are accessible to everyone. Through the years, it has expanded and met far more goals, becoming the most influential preservation organisation in England. Although much restructuring and organising continues, the needs set by the original founders have been met.

THE ENGLISH HERITAGE

The English Heritage was established in 1984 through the National Heritage Act. The purpose of the act is to ensure the protection and responsibility of England's involvement, and importantly, to promote public enjoyment of heritage sites, with Historic England's responsibility for advising the government.

These changes were created as a successor to older bodies and the responsibility to advise the government. They also foster public interest in all aspects of the historic environment in England and Wales.

In 2015, English Heritage underwent significant restructuring into two entities as follows:

a) A charitable foundation will manage the properties that open to the public

b) A separate body will oversee planning controls on properties owned by others

The English Heritage Trust, which manages the National Heritage Historic England, is a public advisory body responsible for heritage protection.

THE NATIONAL TRUST AND ENGLISH HERITAGE TRUST

Both have distinct responsibilities. English Heritage's focus is on archaeological sites and ancient monuments. National Trust's responsibilities are a continuation of their long-standing commitment with a focus on:

a) Country Houses

b) Landscapes

c) Visitor Engagement

d) Education

e) Community Involvements

English Heritage has a predominant history and culture involving archaeology. This involves archaeological research and excavations, as well as preservation of archaeological sites and collections while collaborating with universities.

OPEN ACCESS LAND UK

THE COUNTRYSIDE AND RIGHTS OF WAY ACT (UK) 2000

The Countryside Right of Way Act provides for people to walk, run, explore, and watch wildlife. For those who have not travelled abroad for the purpose of camping, walking, etc, it is always best to check regulations before you begin. Regulation orders are made for the purpose of preserving natural beauty.

For many years, there were large areas of private English heritage land that were not permitted to be used by people such as hikers. But after years of lobbying, in 2000, a new act called *CROW 2000* opened many areas. The result is that CROW gives a public right of access to land mapped as 'open country,' including mountain, moor, heath, down, and registered common land. This act opens as much as three million acres. While CROW clarifies much as to what is allowed and where, however, there are other rules, such as:

a) Hikers do not have the right to walk over agricultural land or other 'private lands' unless the owner is a 'right-of-way holder.' This is an owner who provides land to become a trail or right of way for a walker and is paid by the government to maintain this trail.

b) Or on the property of a 'dedicated' landowner who has at least 90 years left on their leases.

For walkers, use gates, stiles, or gaps in field boundaries if you are able. Be sure that the gates are left fastened.

You can contact the Open Access Centre for information about open access land at: open.acess@naturalengland.org.uk

Telephone: **0300 060 2091**

THE DOMESDAY BOOK

In some of the writing in this book, especially when discussing the churches and their history, the Domesday Book is mentioned. This is frequently a way of providing the reader with an idea of the age of a building.

The Domesday Book provides a detailed record of land ownership and resources across England. It was compiled in 1086 by the order of William the Conqueror, following the Norman conquest of 1066. This record acts as a survey of land, detailing who owned what property, how much they held, the value of the holding, and so much more. This provided valuable and crucial information for taxation and administrative purposes. The bottom line: the Domesday Book is a detailed survey and valuation of landed property at the end of the 11th century. In simple terms, this is an early census.

In later times, English counties, such as Norfolk (where I was born), Suffolk, and Essex, were not included. When this was realised, there was a more detailed version of what is called The Little

Domesday that was created. Today, the Domesday Book is confined within five volumes.

How do we use this survey/census today?

The Domesday Book is accessible and is used by historians and researchers. It has been digitised and made available online via the National Archives in the United Kingdom.

As noted earlier, it provides an estimate of the history of so many of England's churches, houses, and many historical places.

How accurate is it? How was the information obtained and used?

While we question this, we must recognise what a great and difficult effort it was.

THE WALKING MADONNA

The Walking Madonna is a statue sculpted by Elisabeth Frink, the sculptor known as 'one of Britain's best post-war sculptors and figurative artists,' who, interestingly, very seldom sculpted any female forms, although the Walking Madonna's subject matter of masculine strength, struggle, and aggression clearly came through in the statue. The poem was beautifully written by Nicola Slee, and it perfectly describes the feeling that came to me when holding the hand of Madonna.

Nicola Slee is a published poet and acclaimed author in the fields of feminist and practical theology, spirituality, and prayer. This movement re-evaluates religious scriptures and practices from a feminist perspective with an aim to create inclusive and just religious communities.

THE POEM

For centuries, they have been hidden away under
canopies of copious draperies. Always, she is static,
seated, or standing. You cannot imagine her
moving, as if all her joints had seized up.

But Frink has her striding, not merely ambling, but
positively hiking out of the cathedral cloister. She's
wiry; she's lean. She's taking enormous paces away
from the towering edifice.

Undeterred by tourists, she is leaving the sacred
places. She's heading for Salisbury Plain, that vast
open space she's been denied for centuries. She's
had enough of bishops and choir boys paying her
scant attention, of ladies in large hats averting their
faces from her gaze.

She's getting out where she can breathe, where she can throw back her head and drink in the pure, wind-whipped air, filling her lungs full. She's getting ready to holler. She's hitching up her skirts, getting them out of the way, no longer hampered by yardage of feminine frippery. She's got her walking boots on and thick socks.

She's got her rucksack with little needs for the journey: water, some provisions, a compass, a whistle.

She's heading for the hill country, on her way to Cousin Elizabeth. She's making for female company. But first, she's off on her own.

She wants to hear her thoughts in her own head, undisturbed. She wants to listen to the sound of her body moving; she knows where she is going. She trusts her own two legs that will carry her there: her two purposeful legs taut with their untested strength.